Chicago's Dream, a World's Treasure

The Art Institute of Chicago, 1893-1993

TROCADERO.

Chicago's Dream, a World's Treasure

The Art Institute of Chicago, 1893-1993

NEIL HARRIS

EDITED BY TERI J. EDELSTEIN

AFTERWORD BY JAMES N. WOOD

THE ART INSTITUTE OF CHICAGO

This book has been prepared in conjunction with the exhibition "Chicago's Dream, a World's Treasure: The Art Institute of Chicago, 1893–1993," held at The Art Institute of Chicago from November 1, 1993, to January 9, 1994.

Robert V. Sharp, Associate Director of Publications
Michael Sittenfeld, Editor
Katherine Houck Fredrickson, Senior Production Manager
Manine Rosa Golden, Production Assistant
Research assistance by Margo Hobbs Thompson
Editorial assistance by Kathleen Hartman

Designed by Three Communication Design, Chicago
Typeset in Centaur and Univers 67
Color separations by Professional Graphics, Rockford, Illinois
Printed by CS Graphics, Singapore

The photographs were produced by the Department of Imaging and Technical Services, Alan B. Newman, Executive Director. Principal photography by Chester Brummel, Christopher K. Gallagher, Robert Hashimoto, and Leslie Umberger of the Department of Imaging and Technical Services, and Nancy K. Finn of the Department of Textiles. Photographic research assistance by Annie Morse.

All photographs reproduced in this book are in the collections of The Art Institute of Chicago, except for the historical photograph on the cover and frontispiece by J. W. Taylor, 1892/93, courtesy of the Chicago Historical Society. The historical postcards of the Art Institute have been drawn from the collections of the Department of Archives.

Many of the archival photographs reproduced in this book were collected and catalogued as part of The Art Institute of Chicago Digital Imaging Negative Project, which has been funded through a generous grant from the Samuel H. Kress Foundation. These negatives were digitized on a Sharp JX-600 scanner and image-processed in Adobe Photoshop on a Macintosh Quadra computer to create duotones.

ISBN: 0-86559-121-0

Contents

NEIL HARRIS

The Art Institute of Chicago, 1893–1993

Centennials are hospitable opportunities for reminiscence and celebration, but they are meant to occur only once. Having already celebrated its hundredth birthday in 1979, The Art Institute of Chicago cannot easily do so again in 1993. Instead, its move across Michigan Avenue to a new building is now being marked.

This second centennial has its own significance. The Art Institute's actual foundation as the Chicago Academy of Fine Arts—a name it held until 1882—took place almost midway between two great bursts of cultural and philanthropic energy in Chicago. In combination they gave the city historical societies, universities, theaters, libraries, science museums, hospitals, settlement houses, civic clubs, and a great exposition. Despite continuities and parallels, the two eras expressed real differences of scale and intention.

Begun not long before the fevered flowering of Chicago's cultural ambition and shortly after its anticipatory statements, the Art Institute testified in important ways to the earlier era of philanthropy. Its

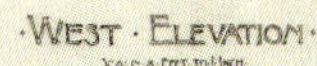

Plate 1. John Wellborn Root (American, 1850–1891). *First Study for The Art Institute of Chicago,* c. 1890 (unexecuted), delineated by Paul Lautrup. Watercolor and pencil on paper. Gift of John Wellborn Root, Jr.

Figure 1 (top). Shepley, Rutan and Coolidge, architects. West elevation of the Art Institute, working drawing, 1892. Ink on linen.

concern with art education and regional needs endorsed the didactic spirit and local aims characterizing older institutions like the Chicago Academy of Sciences and the Chicago Historical Society. For over fifty years the Middle West had been dotted by just such serious-minded collections absorbed by the need to preserve regional history, instruct aspiring practitioners, and promote scientific and literary ideals.

But the Art Institute was pushed just as inexorably toward the later period and the expansive mood typified by newcomers like the Auditorium Building, the University of Chicago, and the Chicago Symphony Orchestra. Here intense ambition, cosmopolitan claims, rigorous professionalism, and a delight in well-publicized display replaced or at least supplemented the local, service-oriented, semi-utilitarian spirit of the earlier day. The new institutions promised to bring the city international attention, and more than simply attention, acclaim. They constituted the gauntlet Chicago had thrown down before its older sisters on the East Coast, most notably the larger, richer, and still more important New York.

Construction of the 1893 building was as apt a symbol of these expanding aspirations as anything else the Art Institute did. The decision to build it–in a certain style, of a certain size, and at a certain place–suggested that the trustees and managers of the institution had determined thus to objectify their sense of art's transcendent idealism and the imperial status of the surrounding city.

Buildings are not always destiny. Many organizations have confronted unhappy conceits and impossible constrictions in arrangements they confidently expected would last for several generations. And it is often

Figure 2. The Art Institute of Chicago, looking northeast across Michigan Avenue, c. 1894.

possible to relieve such problems, to expand, to renovate. Sometimes, even to move. Museums, considerably less mobile than law firms, appliance stores, and used car lots, are veteran expanders. The original 50,000 square feet on Michigan at Adams of 1893 have, 100 years later, become 400,000 square feet in a maze of buildings stretching from Monroe down to Jackson. At least half a dozen architectural firms, with differing approaches and philosophies, have contributed to the present complex.

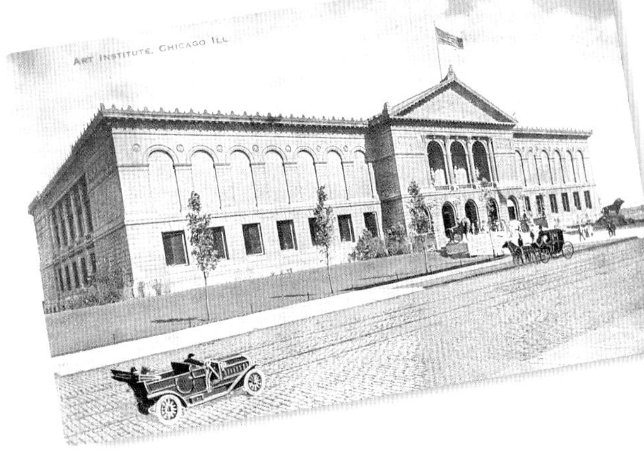

Veiled by the daily steam of hundreds of hissing locomotives, the Art Institute's lonely splendor symbolized to some the fate of high culture in Chicago.

But the original structure has emerged as an enduring icon, a more expressive institutional statement than most of its satellite additions. The new edifice captured a sense of cultural adventurism that was both continental and nationalistic. It was connected through its funding to that most flamboyant of contemporary events, the triumphalist World's Columbian Exposition of 1893. The managers of the Columbian Exposition, hoping briefly that the Art Institute might join the new Arts Palace in Jackson Park, agreed to subsidize part of the construction cost in exchange for using the building as a downtown site for learned and professional meetings during the fair. The construction of the new building was also linked to public authority and continental expansion because of its location on park land presented to the people of Chicago by the Illinois and Michigan Canal commissioners and, ultimately, through federal grant. Thus the specific site was joined to the march of American nationhood in an intimate and direct fashion.

The Michigan Avenue building, with its neoclassical mimicry of European institutions and its majestic invocation of Italian Renaissance grandeur, stood squarely opposite the honeycombed headquarters of Chicago's industrial and commercial interests. The iron rails of the Illinois Central, today enveloped by the Art Institute, then loomed along one side of the building. The west side was defined by the city's most elegant downtown avenue, and just beyond lay the downtown maelstrom. Veiled by the daily steam of hundreds of hissing locomotives, the Institute's lonely splendor symbolized to some the fate of high culture in Chicago. Yes, it lay in the heart of the city, but would it become an outpost rather than a central node? To answer that question decades of history would be necessary.

Ensconced in its new home, the Art Institute was soon emphasizing inclusion and accessibility. By the early twentieth century both attendance and membership had outstripped every other art museum in America. It farmed objects out to schools and to Park District field houses. The largest art school in the United States, whose night classes served local workers, was part of the enterprise. Dozens of clubs and societies met in its increasingly crowded spaces. It sponsored regional shows for contemporary American artists and, however reluctantly on some levels, hosted an occasional challenge to traditional art mores like the visiting Armory Show of 1913.

All this was closely tied to the Art Institute's physical position. Located not only in America's second largest city, but, for a while in the early twentieth century, the fourth largest city in the world, the Art Institute was Chicago's only art museum. Its responsibilities seemed unbounded: to ancient, medieval, and modern Europe; to decorative, graphic, and plastic art; to the West, the Middle East, the Far East, and America; to artists, businessmen, advertisers, commercial designers, school teachers, and boosters.

Figure 3. View of the Ryerson Library at the Art Institute, c. 1916.

The word institute is, if less august a term, more comprehensive than museum. It suggests system, purpose, organized intention, a broader range of options and improvements than the filtered communion of a home for the muses. The name seemed especially appropriate to its place and time. Chicagoans claimed to be forming a new kind of urban society, leavening the vital but brutal confrontation of forces that created the modern city with a level of civic cultural participation that hearkened back to Renaissance Italy for inspiration. In these early years Art Institute trustees were, for the most part, fully representative of the industrial and commercial empires that had, as it were, called Chicago into being. Politically conservative, personally authoritarian, and, in some cases, socially exclusive, many attached great importance to their appointed task of combining commerce and culture.

How well the Art Institute has balanced its dual allegiances – professional instruction and secular display, aesthetic appreciation and specialized connoisseurship, local responsibility and international ambition, traditional taste and contemporary patronage, critical authority and artistic rebellion, social commitment and introspective aestheticism – is a judgment that depends on one's vantage point. This book, even though it moves to a generally chronological beat, emphasizes this process. The life of an institution is shaped by continuing negotiations among its managers, supporters, and staff, and by their contesting interpretations of its mandate. Personnel and perception are dynamic categories. Tastes change; elites shift; curators move; attendance fluctuates; opinions clash. But every moment does seek to express some sense of priority, distinguishing itself from its predecessors through its own special agenda. A century of activity

REYNOLDS
VIOLLET LE DUC
LEONARDO
WINCKELMAN

Figure 4. The Elizabeth Hammond Stickney Room on the second floor of the Art Institute opened in 1899. This gallery, designed by Chicago's most renowned interior decorator, Louis J. Millet, featured a mosaic floor and a green marble dado beneath vibrant red walls.

includes dissent and disagreement along with a search for disciplined traditions. Embedded in this past are ironies and paradoxes, broad tolerances and narrow bigotries, sometimes lying side by side.

The Art Institute's deep identification with the life of Chicago and the Midwest, the fierce pride it has elicited (and demanded) from donors and supporters, its characteristic self-promotion, and its efforts, more than once in every generation, to reinvent its mission and its methods, are among

The Art Institute's deep identification with the life of Chicago and the Midwest and the fierce pride it has elicited from donors and supporters are among the ingredients that have supplied its special character.

the ingredients that have supplied its special character. But its collections contain important clues, not only to what it has become but also to why it is here. The tens of thousands of objects offer rich insights into personal obsession, aesthetic taste, social conformity, and fearless risk taking. Their concentrated presence evokes generations of collectors, connoisseurs, cataloguers, and antiquarians, whose values and concerns were often stubbornly disparate. In displaying these selected artworks as part of its anniversary celebration, the Art Institute opens to view not only the range of its possessions, but also the blend of personal, impersonal, intentional, and unanticipated forces that together, over time, create a collection. In their diversity and multiple meanings these objects expose the archaeology of desire and possession that constitutes the heart of any great museum. But in their special combination, their emphases and exclusions, they express only one place, The Art Institute of Chicago. How and why they arrived here must occupy other narratives. But that they made the journey at all remains an occasion for marvel. And, after allowing some time for analysis and self-criticism, for celebration as well.

Figure 5. Interior view of the Art Institute's Blackstone Hall, c. 1905. This enormous gallery, which opened in 1903, housed more than 150 plaster casts of artworks.

The Original Museum

At the start, collection quality was not an overwhelming concern for Art Institute organizers. Instruction was. Authenticity and distinction, while not to be dismissed, counted less than coverage and reputation. Casts and photographs could supplement the initial inventory, in the interest of unfolding the vast yet clearly organized panorama of art as accepted evolutionary theory had mapped it. Connection and descent could be as significant an artistic signifier as it was a social credential. But even in their early years the Art Institute's galleries could startle, amuse, arouse, or awe visitors just emerging into an era of lavish reproduction. However condescending later generations might feel toward these first gatherings, their search represented a quest for approval and refinement intense beyond easy imaginings. And, as children of fashion, they set a pattern which would continue in the future.

Figure 6. Lobby of the Michigan Avenue entrance, 1903/05, looking south into the galleries of Roman casts (the present location of the Museum Shop).

Plaster-cast reproductions of artworks were common in European and American museums in the late nineteenth century, and the Art Institute was no exception. From 1884 through the early 1950s, the Art Institute exhibited plaster reproductions of Greek and Roman, Renaissance, and modern sculpture, as well as casts of architectural elements in an enormous gallery known as Blackstone Hall.

Figures 7 and 8. Japanese print exhibition designed by Frank Lloyd Wright at the Art Institute, 1908. This exhibition displayed 655 Japanese prints, many of which eventually entered the museum's permanent collection.

Plate 2. Kitagawa Utamaro (Japanese, 1753–1806). *Woman Holding a Comb,* c. 1798. Woodblock print. Clarence Buckingham Collection.

Figure 9. View of the "International Exhibition of Modern Art," more commonly known as the "Armory Show," at the Art Institute, 1913. The third painting from the left, bottom row, is André Derain's *Forest at Martigues* (pl. 4), which is now in the Art Institute's permanent collection.

Plate 3. Pablo Picasso (Spanish, 1881–1973). *Head of Fernande Olivier,* 1909. Bronze. Alfred Stieglitz Collection.

Plate 4. André Derain (French, 1880–1954). *Forest at Martigues,* c. 1908. Oil on canvas. Arthur Jerome Eddy Memorial Collection.

The international exhibition known as the "Armory Show" of 1913 at the Art Institute presented a wide range of works by European and American modern artists. It attracted huge crowds and aroused enormous public controversy with the display of works by some of the foremost members of the European avant-garde, including Pablo Picasso, Georges Braque, Marcel Duchamp, and Francis Picabia.

Figure 10. Henry Field Memorial Collection Gallery at the Art Institute, c. 1916. The large painting in the middle of the far wall is Jules Breton's *Song of the Lark* (pl. 5).

Plate 5 (right). Jules Breton (French, 1827–1906). *The Song of the Lark,* 1884. Oil on canvas. Henry Field Memorial Collection.

Figure 11. Eleanor Roosevelt at a ceremony honoring Jules Breton's *Song of the Lark* (pl. 5), during the Century of Progress exhibition at the Art Institute, July 10, 1934. *The Song of the Lark* was voted the most popular painting in America in a contest conducted by the *Chicago Daily News.*

Plate 6. Rembrandt Harmensz. van Rijn (Dutch, 1606–1669) or follower. *Young Woman at an Open Half-Door,* 1645. Oil on canvas. Mr. and Mrs. Martin A. Ryerson Collection. This painting was formerly in the Demidoff Collection, and was purchased with funds provided by the Ryersons.

Figure 12. Second-floor gallery near the Grand Staircase, c. 1917. The large canvas on the left is the Art Institute's most significant Old Master painting, El Greco's *Assumption of the Virgin* (1577), which entered the museum's collection in 1906.

From its earliest days, the Art Institute acquired significant masterpieces of European and American art. The museum signaled its intention to build a formidable collection of Old Master paintings when it purchased from the Demidoff Collection in 1894 fourteen Dutch and Flemish masterpieces by such artists as Frans Hals, Meindert Hobbema, and Rembrandt.

Figure 13. Art Institute guards on duty, 1917.

Figure 14. Art handlers moving sculpture through the museum, 1910.

Figure 15. Gallery with plaster casts of Egyptian and Assyrian sculpture at the Art Institute, 1917.

Plate 7. Egyptian. *Mummy Mask,* c. 100 B.C. Cartonnage (gummed linen and plaster), gold foil, and paint. W. M. Willner Fund.

Figure 16. View from the southeast of the Art Institute, c. 1910.

Figure 17. In 1922, the Burnham Library of the Art Institute commissioned from the Chicago architect Louis H. Sullivan a set of drawings representing his theories of architectural ornament (see pl. 8). These drawings were featured in the Chicago Architectural Exhibition League show of May 1924, at which time the Art Institute mounted a memorial exhibition on Sullivan, who died on April 14th of that year. The centerpiece of the memorial exhibition was a teller's wicket from the National Farmers Bank in Owatonna, Minnesota, acquired by the museum in 1908.

Plate 8. Louis H. Sullivan (American, 1856–1924). *Untitled Ornamental Design,* 1923, plate 19 from *A System of Architectural Ornament,* 1924. Pencil on Strathmore paper. Commissioned by The Art Institute of Chicago.

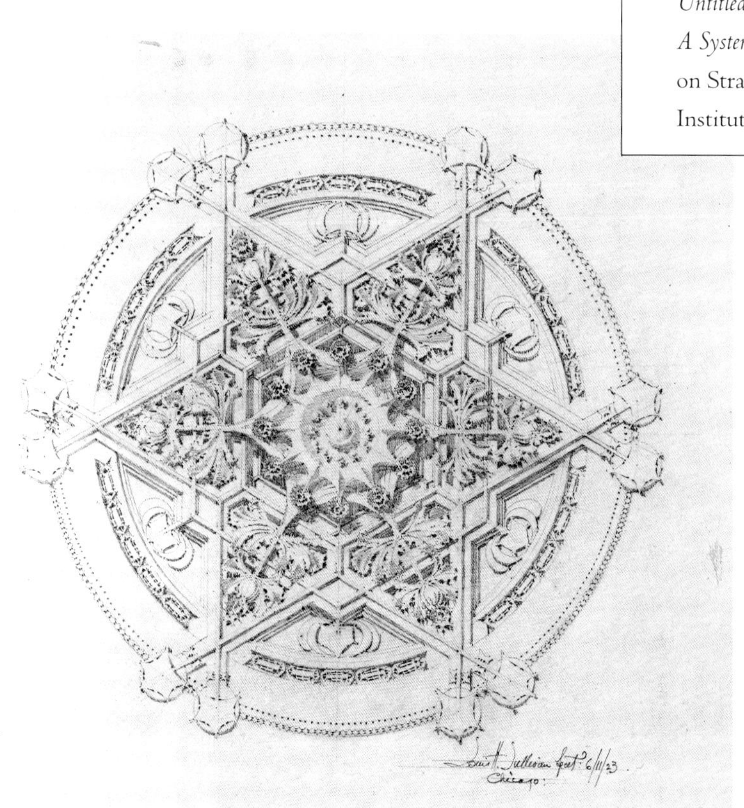

Figure 18. Michigan Avenue entrance to the Art Institute at night, looking north, 1917.

Determining Tastes

Most of what a museum possesses are gifts rather than purchases. Thus its holdings reflect what collectors have happened to buy and have been willing to donate. A few dozen people were finally responsible for much of what fills these galleries. Their interests, tastes, friendships, and local loyalties, to say nothing of their psychological profiles and social connections, shaped their choices.

But they cannot be thought of as passive victims of larger forces. Often independent, sometimes iconoclastic, increasingly cosmopolitan, the patrons of the first quarter century began to transform the Art Institute, not from pedagogical or civic ambitions, but because the art accumulating in their own homes began its journey to the museum itself. However different their immediate aims and intentions, they developed their own expertise and standards of acceptability, and they would make the Art Institute bear witness to them. These collectors were amateurs, at a time when art professionals were few and far between. They took advice, but not direction. In so doing they established a special personality for their favored museum, strong in some areas, weak or nonexistent in others. Even today the museum's character reflects the enthusiasms of donors whose collecting ceased more than sixty years ago.

The bequest of fifty-two paintings from the collection of Bertha Honoré Palmer (1849-1918) was presented to the Art Institute in 1922. This extraordinary group of works, known as the Potter Palmer Collection, ensured that the Art Institute could offer its visitors one of the foremost installations of Impressionist paintings in the world.

Plate 9. Claude Monet (French, 1840–1926). *Grainstacks (Sunset, Snow Effect)*, 1891. Oil on canvas. Potter Palmer Collection.

Plate 10. Pierre Auguste Renoir (French, 1841–1919). *Jugglers at the Circus Fernando,* 1878–79. Oil on canvas. Potter Palmer Collection.

Plate 11. Edouard Manet (French, 1832–1883). *The Races at Longchamp,* 1864. Oil on canvas. Potter Palmer Collection.

Bertha Honoré Palmer was a prominent Chicago socialite who served as the president of the Board of Lady Managers at the World's Columbian Exposition in 1893. Through her friendship with the artist Mary Cassatt, she became an early and ardent champion of Impressionism, and collected works by Monet, Renoir, Manet, Degas, and others.

Plate 12. Edgar Degas (French, 1834–1917). *The Morning Bath,* c. 1890. Pastel on paper. Potter Palmer Collection.

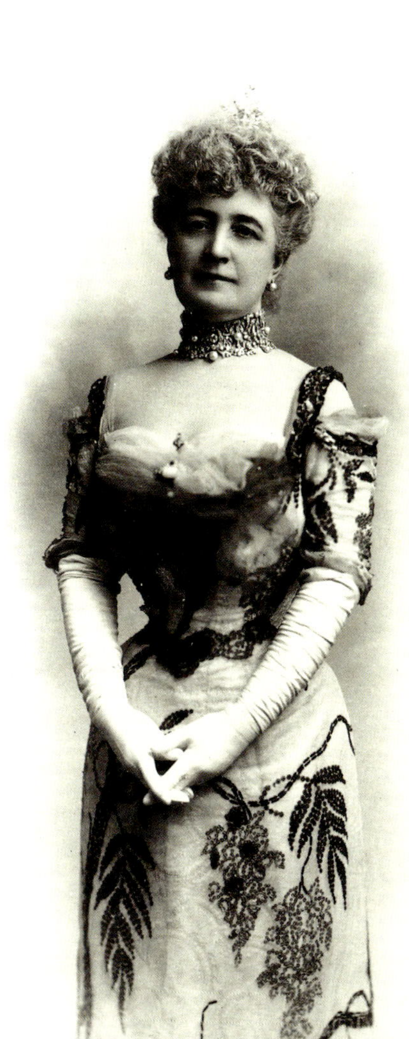

Figure 19. Bertha Honoré Palmer.

Figure 20. Martin A. Ryerson also collected Impressionist paintings, and he is shown in this photograph visiting Claude Monet in the artist's garden at Giverny, France, in June 1920.

Martin A. Ryerson (1856-1932) was perhaps the single most important donor of works of art to the Art Institute, including masterpieces of European and American painting from the fifteenth to twentieth centuries, as well as textiles, prints and drawings, Asian art, and European decorative arts.

Plate 13. Claude Monet. *Water Lilies,* 1906. Oil on canvas. Mr. and Mrs. Martin A. Ryerson Collection.

Plate 14. Winslow Homer (American, 1836–1910). *After the Tornado, Texas,* 1899. Watercolor on paper. Mr. and Mrs. Martin A. Ryerson Collection.

Plate 15. Giovanni di Paolo (Italian, c. 1403–1482/83). *The Life of Saint John the Baptist: Saint John in the Wilderness,* c. 1450 or 1460. Tempera on panel. Mr. and Mrs. Martin A. Ryerson Collection.

The extraordinary collection of Japanese woodblock prints amassed by Chicago businessman Clarence Buckingham (1854-1913) was presented to the Art Institute in 1925 by his sister Kate Sturges Buckingham (1858-1937), whose donations of endowment funds and countless works of art—ceramics, Chinese bronzes, Japanese and Chinese paintings—were to make her the most prominent contributor to the Art Institute's Asian art collection.

Plate 16. Chinese. *Flowerpot,* Jin dynasty, twelfth century. Jun ware, stoneware with opaque reddish purple glaze. Lucy Maud Buckingham Collection.

Figure 21. Kate Sturges Buckingham.

Plate 17. Chinese. *Tripod Wine Vessel (Jia),* Shang dynasty, twelfth century B.C. Bronze. Lucy Maud Buckingham Collection.

Plate 18. Swiss. *Hanging Entitled "The Lovers,"* 1490/1500. Linen, wool, and silk, slit and double interlocking tapestry weave. Gift of Kate S. Buckingham.

Plate 19. Chinese. *Scissors,* Tang dynasty, first half of eighth century. Silver with chased and ringmatted decoration. Lucy Maud Buckingham Collection.

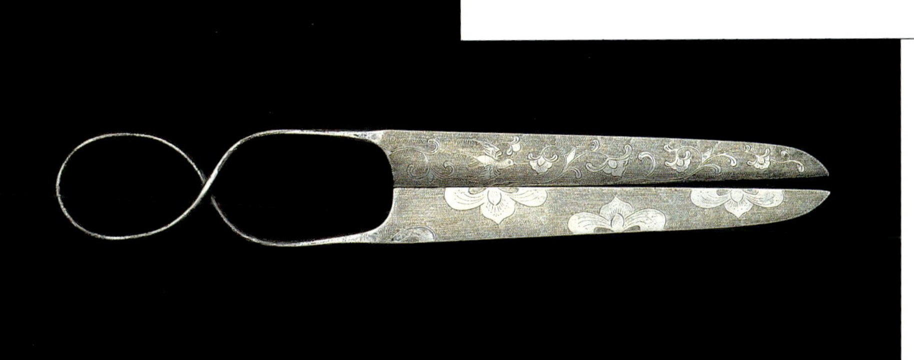

Plate 20. Georges Seurat (French, 1859–1891). *Oil Sketch for the "Grande Jatte,"* 1884. Oil on panel. Gift of Mary and Leigh Block.

Transforming Masterpieces

"Our present policy of acquiring works of art," Robert Harshe remarked in 1921, "depending as it does on what is offered to us . . . leads us into casual and haphazard acquisitions." However wonderful such haphazard acquisitions might often be, and however limited purchase funds usually were, the Art Institute acknowledged the need to shape its own destiny by individual purchase. And several donors created their own special funds to acquire exceptional works or to fill out special collections. Over time, these efforts produced a series of individual objects of extraordinary intensity and broad appeal. The purchase of a group of Old Masters from the Demidoff Collection in 1894 began the pattern; the 1906 acquisition of the El Greco altarpiece confirmed it; and the 1926 addition of the *Grande Jatte* sanctified it. With this determined quest for specific masterpieces, the Art Institute, and a few insistent donors, acquired for themselves those signature pieces whose beauty or rarity built both reputation abroad and devotion at home.

Plate 21. Georges Seurat. *A Sunday on La Grande Jatte–1884,* 1884–86. Oil on canvas. Helen Birch Bartlett Memorial Collection.

Widely considered one of the greatest paintings of the nineteenth century, Georges Seurat's Sunday on La Grande Jatte—1884 *has been the best-known painting in the Art Institute's collection since it was donated to the museum in 1926 by Frederic Clay Bartlett in honor of his second wife, Helen Birch Bartlett.*

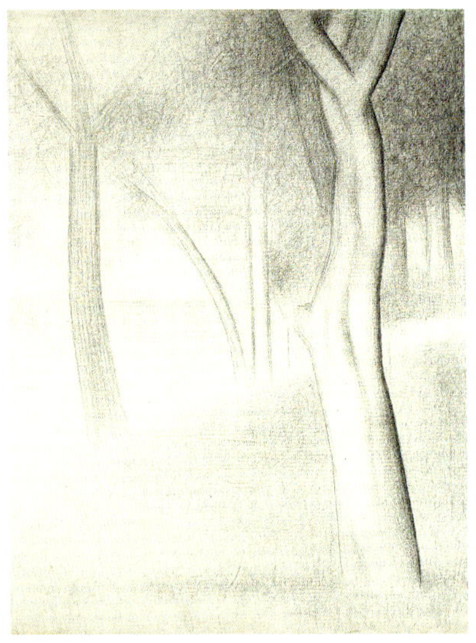

Plate 22. Georges Seurat. *Tree,* 1884. Black conté crayon on white laid paper. Helen Regenstein Collection.

Plate 23. Georges Seurat. *A Sunday on La Grande Jatte—1884* (detail).

Figure 22. Actor Charles Laughton standing beside Georges Seurat's *Sunday on La Grande Jatte—1884,* at the Art Institute, 1935.

Figure 23. A wintertime view from the southeast of the Art Institute's McKinlock Court, 1948.

The Professional's Role

Mediating among various constituencies – donors, visitors, collectors, trustees – curators, conservators, and administrators have steadily increased their sphere of influence during the last seventy years. Where once, in the early twentieth century, trustees and interested amateurs could propose purchases, plan exhibitions, determine installations, or seriously debate questions of authenticity, trained and certified specialists stepped in to make most daily decisions. "Neither the Director nor Curator should be expected to compose the differing opinions of individual Trustees," advised one report in 1921. Installation details should be left "wholly to the Director and his staff."

But professionals do more than simply supply expertise and establish routine. For collectors and for museum visitors, curators can become sources of instruction and inspiration, channeling energy, exemplifying judgment, and outlining standards of coherence and quality that validate and redefine canonical taste. By direction and indirection, by action and example, the professional staff has shaped not only the collection itself but the collector's eye as well.

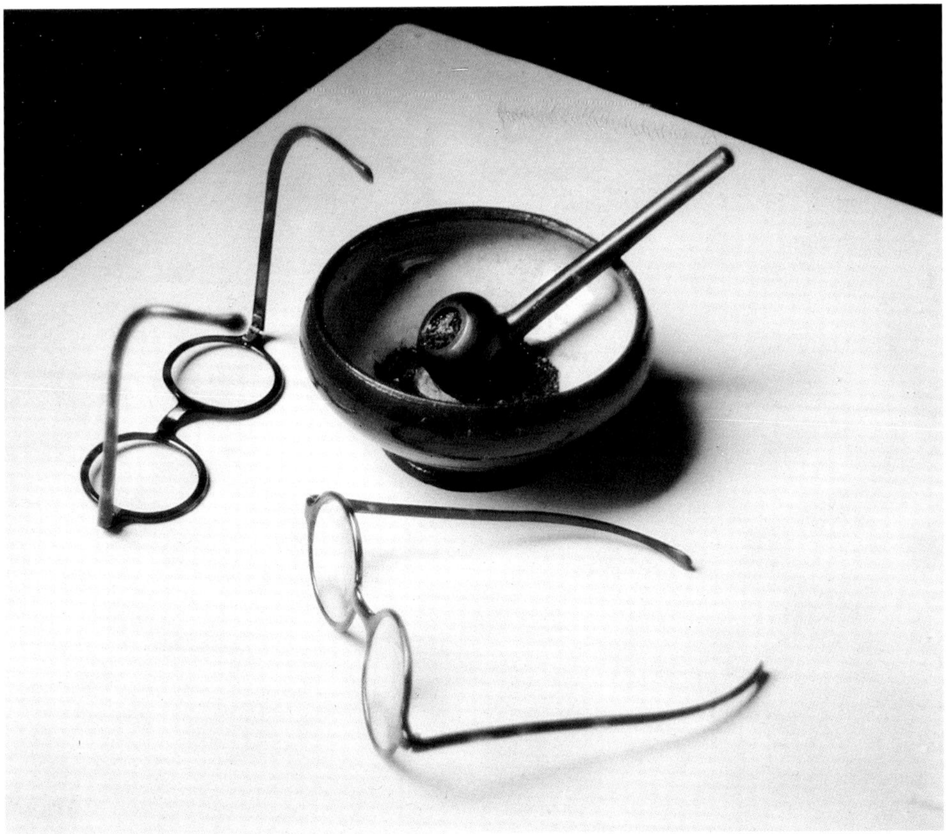

Plate 24. André Kertész (American, born in Hungary, 1894–1985). *Mondrian's Glasses and Pipe,* 1926. Gelatin silver print. Julien Levy Collection, gift of Jean and Julien Levy.

Figure 24 (left). Catalogue for the Art Institute's "Exhibition of Paintings and Sculpture," held as part of the Century of Progress Exposition in 1933.

Plate 25. Max Beckmann (German, 1884–1950). *Carnival in Naples,* 1925, reworked in 1944. Brush with india ink, black crayon, and white chalk on brown wove paper. Gift of Tiffany and Margaret Blake.

Carl O. Schniewind (1900-1957), Curator of Prints and Drawings from 1940 until his death, brought to the Art Institute an unparalleled level of professionalism and connoisseurship. In addition to acquiring a notable collection of French prints and drawings from the seventeenth to nineteenth centuries, he oversaw important acquisitions of modern prints and drawings and organized many exhibitions of contemporary artists, including the first one-man museum show of the works of photographer André Kertész in 1946.

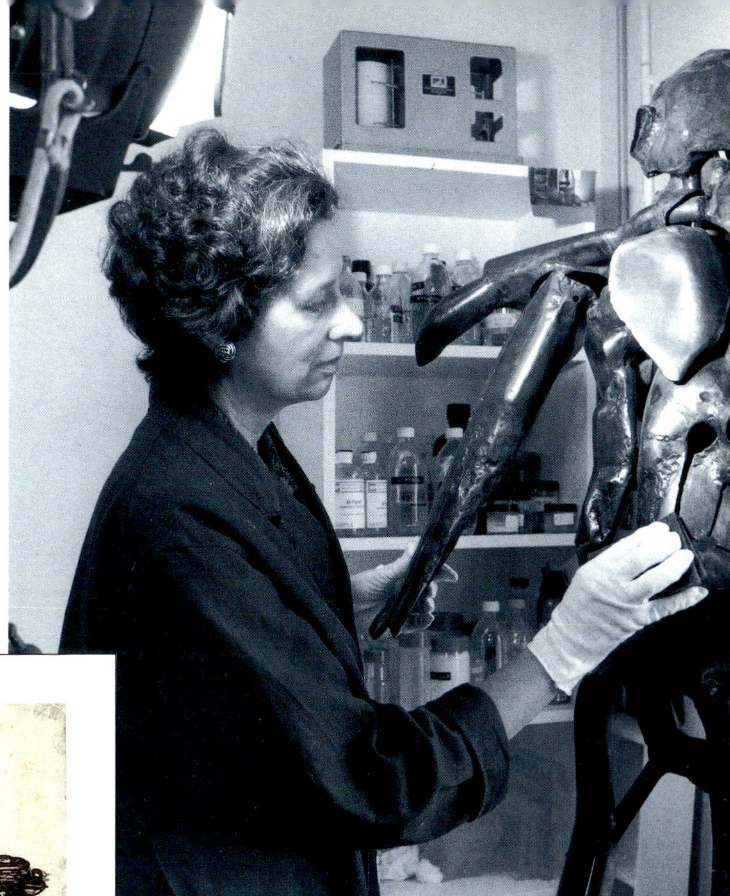

Figure 25. **An Art Institute conservator working on Richard Hunt's sculpture *Hero Construction* (1958).**

Plate 26. Vincent van Gogh (Dutch, 1853–1890). *Corner of a Park at Arles (Tree in a Meadow)*, 1889. Red pen and black ink over charcoal. Gift of Tiffany and Margaret Blake.

Plate 27. Nicolas Poussin (French, 1594–1665). *Landscape with Saint John on Patmos,* 1640. Oil on canvas. A. A. Munger Collection.

Daniel Catton Rich (1904-1976) served as the director of the Art Institute from 1938 to 1958. His tenure was marked by the Art Institute's increased commitment to museum education and the development of a distinguished curatorial and professional staff. He was also responsible for the acquisition of major works by a broad range of artists, from Zurbarán, Guercino, and Poussin, to Matisse, Picasso, and Hopper.

Figure 26. In October 1946, works in the exhibition "Masterpieces of English Painting: Hogarth, Constable, Turner" were brought into the Art Institute through the Michigan Avenue entrance, to the delight of onlookers.

PICTURES

Figure 27. Marc Chagall standing next to his painting *The Praying Jew* (1923) during a visit to the Art Institute in 1958.

Figure 28. Benny Goodman and the Fine Arts Quartet playing the Clarinet Quintet by Brahms in front of Henri Matisse's *Bathers by a River* (1909–16) at the Art Institute, 1960.

Plate 28. Pablo Picasso. *Daniel-Henry Kahnweiler,* 1910. Oil on canvas. Gift of Mrs. Gilbert W. Chapman in memory of Charles B. Goodspeed.

Figure 29. **Georgia O'Keeffe beside her painting *Pelvis III* (1944), which was on loan to the Art Institute when O'Keeffe visited the museum in 1967.**

Figure 30. **Art Institute staff installing Georgia O'Keeffe's *Sky Above Clouds IV* (1965) on the second-floor landing at the end of Gunsaulus Hall, 1991.**

Plate 29. Georgia O'Keeffe (American, 1887–1986). *Black Cross, New Mexico,* 1929. Oil on canvas. The Art Institute of Chicago Purchase Fund.

Plate 30. Frank Lloyd Wright (American, 1867–1959). *Triptych Window from a Niche in the Avery Coonley Playhouse, Riverside, Illinois,* 1912. Clear and colored glass in lead cames. Restricted gift of Dr. and Mrs. Edwin J. DeCosta, and the Walter E. Heller Foundation.

The Expanding Canon

Museum hierarchies bear the patina of established usages and fashionable preferences. They also betray the marks of ethnocentric categorizing. Few would deny the institutional centrality the Art Institute has afforded specific Western traditions of graphic and sculptural art.

Yet while privilege has been unmistakable, it has not been frozen. The expanding net of departments and their changing sets of responsibilities suggest how new media, revised interests, and shifting world views affect the organization of collecting. One era's reproductions are another's authentic art. One generation's foreground is another's background. Debate, reflection, and revision energize both display and accumulation, encouraging the development of new aesthetic criteria and fresh discoveries of mastery.

The museum has collected architectural drawings, models, and fragments since the opening of the Burnham Library of Architecture in 1919, and it has held architectural exhibitions since 1894. But the creation of the Department of Architecture in 1981 solidified Chicago's position as one of the centers of architectural research in the United States.

Plate 31. Robert A. M. Stern (American, born 1939). *Late Entry to Tribune Tower Competition,* 1980. Airbrushed ink on board. Restricted gift of Mr. and Mrs. Thomas J. Eyerman, Mr. and Mrs. David Hilliard, Mrs. Irving F. Stein, Sr., in memory of B. Leo Steif, and Mr. and Mrs. Ben Weese.

Figure 31. Catalogue for the exhibition "Chicago Architecture and Design, 1923–1993," held at the Art Institute in 1993.

Figure 32. View from the southwest of the reconstructed Trading Room at the Art Institute, 1981. Although the Chicago Stock Exchange Building designed by Louis Sullivan and Dankmar Adler was demolished in 1971, the building's historic Trading Room was salvaged and then reconstructed in the Art Institute in 1976–77.

The Department of Africa, Oceania, and the Americas, which was formed in 1957 as the Department of Primitive Art, significantly expanded the scope of the museum's collecting. The department's holdings are as diverse and distinctive as the cultures that produced them, from the farming tribes and kingdoms of the Congo and Niger river systems to the ancient empires of Mesoamerica and the Andean regions.

Plate 32. Nigeria, Yoruba, carved by Olowe of Ise, Ekiti area, Ikere town. *Veranda Post (Opo) Representing an Enthroned King and His Senior Wife,* c. 1914. Carved wood with pigment traces. Major Acquisitions Centennial Endowment.

Plate 33. Zaire, Kuba people. *Mask of a Mythic Ancestor (Mukenga),* late nineteenth/early twentieth century. Wood, beads, cowrie shells, feathers, hair, fiber, skin, and metal. Laura T. Magnuson Endowment.

Figure 33. View of the exhibition "The Ancient Americas: Art from Sacred Landscapes" at the Art Institute, 1992.

Figure 34. Visitors to the "Art Inside Out" exhibition in the Kraft General Foods Education Center at the Art Institute, 1992.

Plate 34. New Mexico, Salado culture. *Ritual Cache Figures,* c. 1350. Stone, wood, cotton, feathers, and pigment. Major Acquisitions Centennial Endowment.

Throughout its history, the Art Institute has dedicated itself to the principle that museum education is one of its major activities. In its programs for adults and children, the Department of Museum Education enhances visitors' understanding, appreciation, and enjoyment of art. The most significant recent event for the department was the opening in 1992 of the Kraft General Foods Education Center.

Figure 35 (top). Kermit the Frog and Miss Piggy of the Muppets presenting their painting *American Gothique* from the "Kermitage Collection" at the opening of the Kraft General Foods Education Center, September 1992.

Figures 36–38. Whether in its lectures or gallery walks, its sponsorship of innovative programs interpreting the museum's collections and exhibitions, or its creative activities for families and children, the Department of Museum Education communicates the significance of art as an expression of the human imagination.

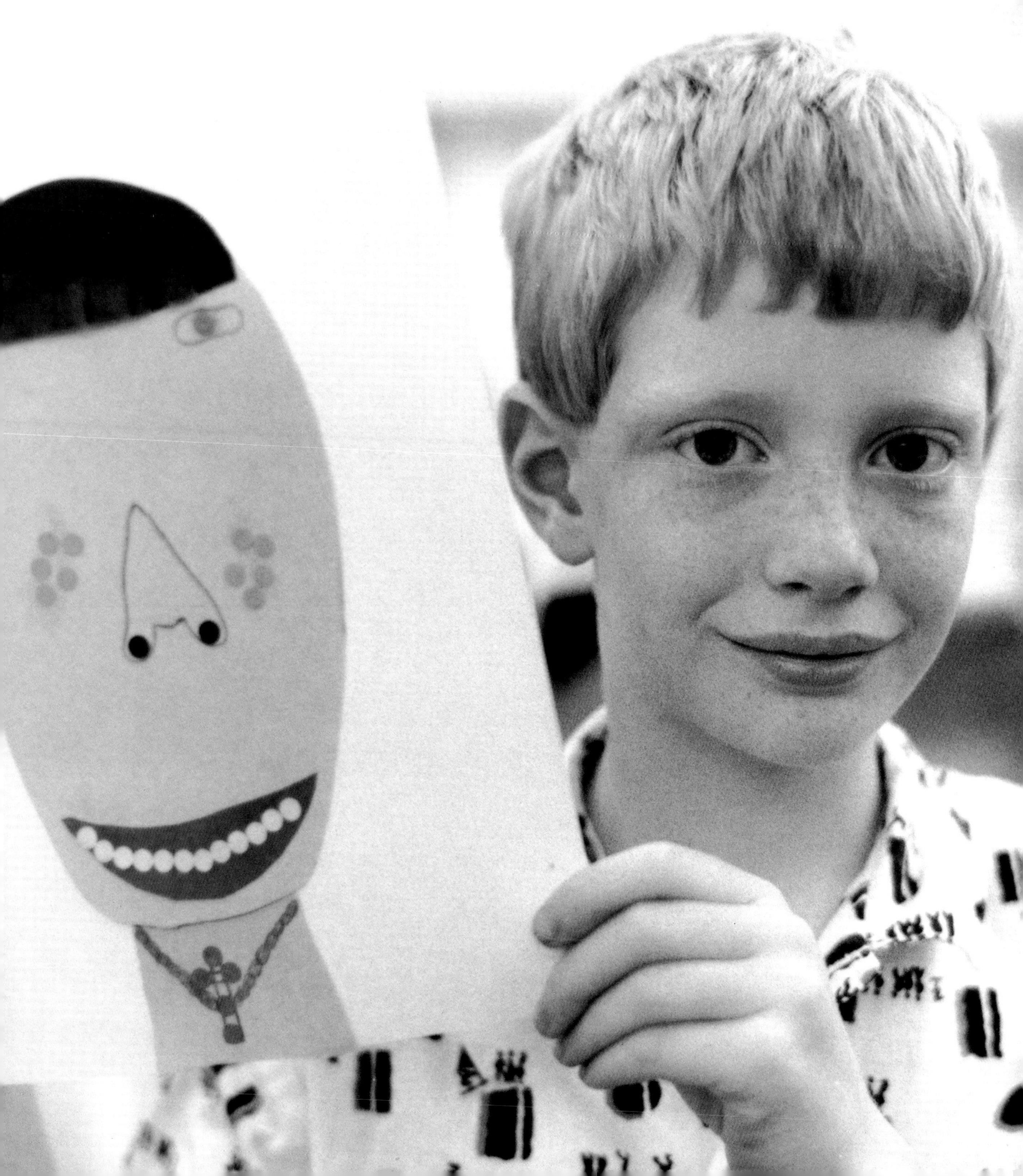

Figure 35. Aerial view of downtown Chicago, 1993. The Art Institute of Chicago, which can be seen in the middleground of this photograph, is situated in Grant Park between Lake Michigan and the skyscrapers of Chicago's Loop.

JAMES N. WOOD
DIRECTOR AND PRESIDENT

Afterword

In 1893 Chicago's leaders erected a magnificent building on the charred rubble that separated the city from the lake. It was a civic monument to the arts symbolically situated in splendid isolation before the burgeoning commercial core of the fastest growing metropolis in the world. It was, however, empty. One hundred years later, it houses our world-renowned permanent collections that, even more than their handsome setting, demonstrate this city's commitment to the arts. Born in the chauvinistic climate of the World's Columbian Exposition, the Art Institute's purpose has continually evolved along with its collections. Its definition of what could be of aesthetic importance has greatly expanded, while its professional standards of quality have become ever more demanding.

The temple-fronted building overlooking Michigan Avenue is a beloved and fitting symbol of the centrality of the arts in Chicago's aspirations, but its symbolism is changing. At the end of the nineteenth century, the challenge was to create a museum where none existed; at the close of

Santa Fe

the twentieth century, it will be to make use of these extraordinary collections to assure that the museum remains at the center of community life. The temple of art was an appropriate symbol for much of our history, but today another classical concept far better expresses the museum's role in society and the purpose that will determine its future. The forum is replacing the temple, providing a common civic space where works of art stimulate both private revelation and public debate. We have been told repeatedly that the electronic media will be the exclusive forum of the future, providing everything to everyone in accessible simulacrum, but I am convinced that a democratic society will and must always demand equal access to the experience of original works of art.

The Art Institute has a bright and demanding future, for the need, and indeed longing, for what we can help provide is growing. As a city, a nation, and a global community, the challenge of learning to live together will be central to our survival. The enduring works of art from around the world that we encounter in this forum share with each of us the insights of their creators and, by doing so, reaffirm our common humanity.